This is the story of sunlight.

The sun's story starts before you or me,
before the Earth,
before the moon.
But for now,
we'll skip ahead a few billion years,
because this is the story of us, too—
how we reached into the sky
and carried the sun home.

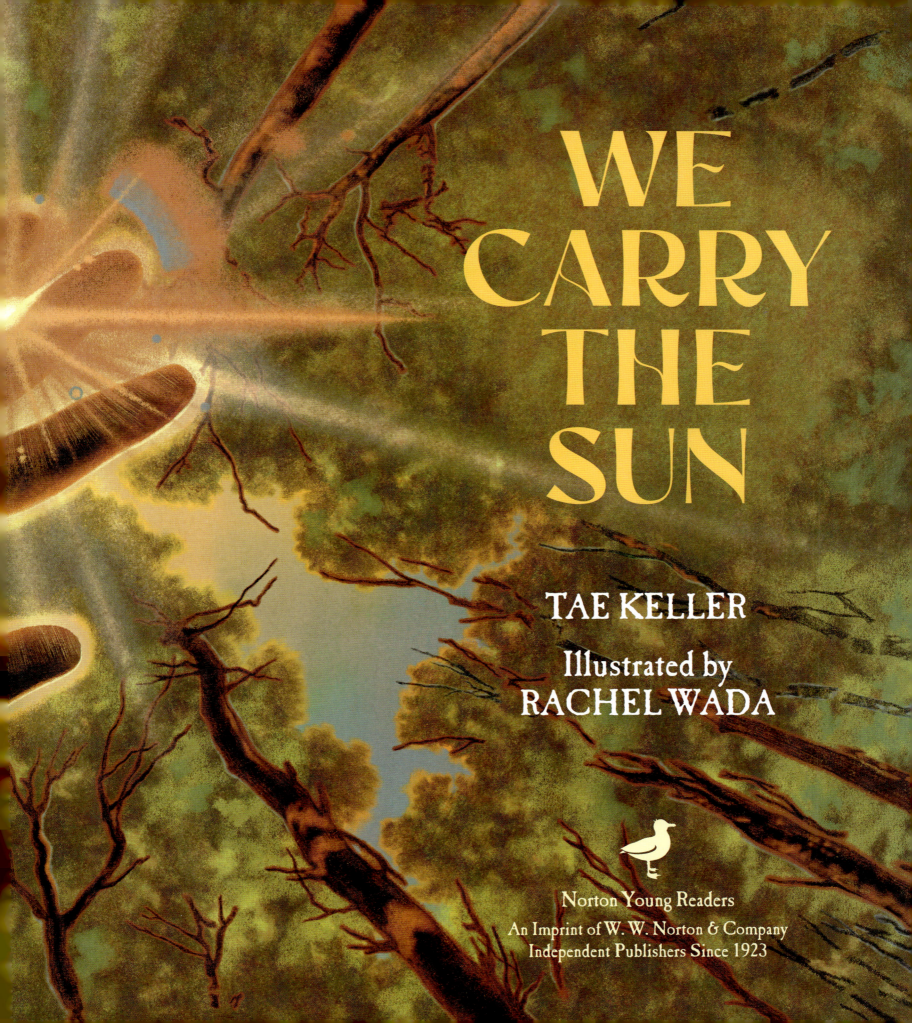

Where does an idea start?

Four billion years after the sun was born,
and six thousand years before you were
(give or take a century),
we humans tilt our faces to the sky,
feel the heat on our skin,
and think,

The sun is incredible.
Look at all it can do.

But what if it could do even more?

Could it keep us warm in our homes,
even as winter frosts the trees outside?

We study the arc of the sun
as it crawls across the sky.
We learn its path,
its habits,
its temperature,
its temperament.

Then we build houses facing south, gathering the sun's rays on bright days so we can stay safe in our homes, though the nights grow cold.

In the 1800s,
we start using coal
to heat homes and factories,
to power steam engines in trains and ships.
We resurrect this coal—
long-dead, fossilized plants,
(fossil fuel)—
from the Earth,
and burn it,
poisoning our planet in the process—
but we don't know that yet.

Some, though, do worry.
Augustin Mouchot, a math teacher in France, wonders,
What if, one day, we run out of coal?
He turns to the sky:
Could we use the sun's power instead?
He researches,
drawing insight and inspiration
from solar experiments years before:
a heat trap, almost like
   a miniature greenhouse,
and a burning mirror,
   used centuries ago in China.

Then he begins to build.

He tries,
fails,
tries again—
combining the two ideas into something new.
The sun reflects off the mirror,
turning the water in the trap into steam,
which powers an engine.

Here it is! he hopes.
An alternative to coal!
A solar steam engine for everyone!

But not so fast.

No matter how hard Augustin works,
coal takes up less space,
provides more power,
and costs less.

The sun sets on Augustin's idea . . .

. . . but not for long.

Two decades later,
a New Yorker named Charles Fritts takes this idea,
and wonders,
*What if we could get energy not just from the sun's heat
but from its light?*
He's heard of a material that sparks in the sun,
a mineral called selenium,
found in soil and sunflower seeds.
He places a thin strip of selenium on a metal sheet,
lays it out in the sun,
and cheers as it makes an electric current!

But how does this work?

Photons—
tiny particles of light—
bounce around, full of energy,
vibrating strongly enough to create electricity.

What an invention!
The world's first solar panel!

Charles's panel is small and light enough
to mount on a roof—
but it's expensive,
and it can hardly power
a bedside lamp.

A bit of a setback. . . .

But humans aren't easily defeated,
and years later,
there's something spectacular in California—

an ostrich farm!

It's a sight people travel far and wide to see,
and they find not only birds . . .
but a new and improved solar engine.

An engineer named Aubrey Eneas
started tweaking and tinkering
with Augustin's design
back in Boston, Massachusetts.
But Boston wasn't sunny enough,
and the solar engine didn't work in the dark.

Now, across the country,
Aubrey has found sun . . . and an audience.

*Come one, come all,
see the birds that capture your imagination,
and the motor that captures the sun!*

Thousands of people flock to Aubrey's machine.
Word spreads.

Aubrey's motor provides all the farm's power—
on a sunny day, at least.

That is incredible. Look at all it can do.

But what if the sun could do even more?

Back in Massachusetts,
a Hungarian immigrant,
scientist Maria Telkes, wonders,
*What if the sun could heat a house
morning and night,
in rain and in shine?*
She calls her friend, architect Eleanor Raymond,
and together,
they build.

Across an ocean, an Israeli woman named Rina Yissar
   tries to give her baby a bath,
but the water is cold,
and she has no fuel for heating.
Turning to the sky, she thinks.
Then she paints an old tub black,
drags it into the sun,
and fills it with water.
Before long, the water is warm.

She hasn't heard what's happening elsewhere,
but she is on to something.
This worked, she tells her engineer husband, Levi.
Can the sun do more?

Levi researches solar water heaters in America.
He adapts the designs for his own country.
Before long, solar heating spreads through the land.
It also becomes popular in Japan, South Africa, and Australia.

Then, in 1955, seventy years after Charles Fritts
　　invented his panel,
something amazing happens.
Scientists at Bell Labs
consider Charles's selenium solar panel,
and wonder, *Can we make this more efficient?*
They tweak, they tinker,
and then, they do.
They replace selenium with *silicon*,
a material found in the Earth's crust.

The electricity from silicon solar panels
can power not just your bedside lamp,
but your whole house.

And not just your whole house . . .

. . . but a spaceship.

Three years later, using Earth-deep silicon,
NASA harnesses the sun's power
to travel *toward* the sun.
They launch Vanguard 1,
the world's first solar-powered satellite.
Vanguard 1 outperforms all previous satellites—
a huge success!

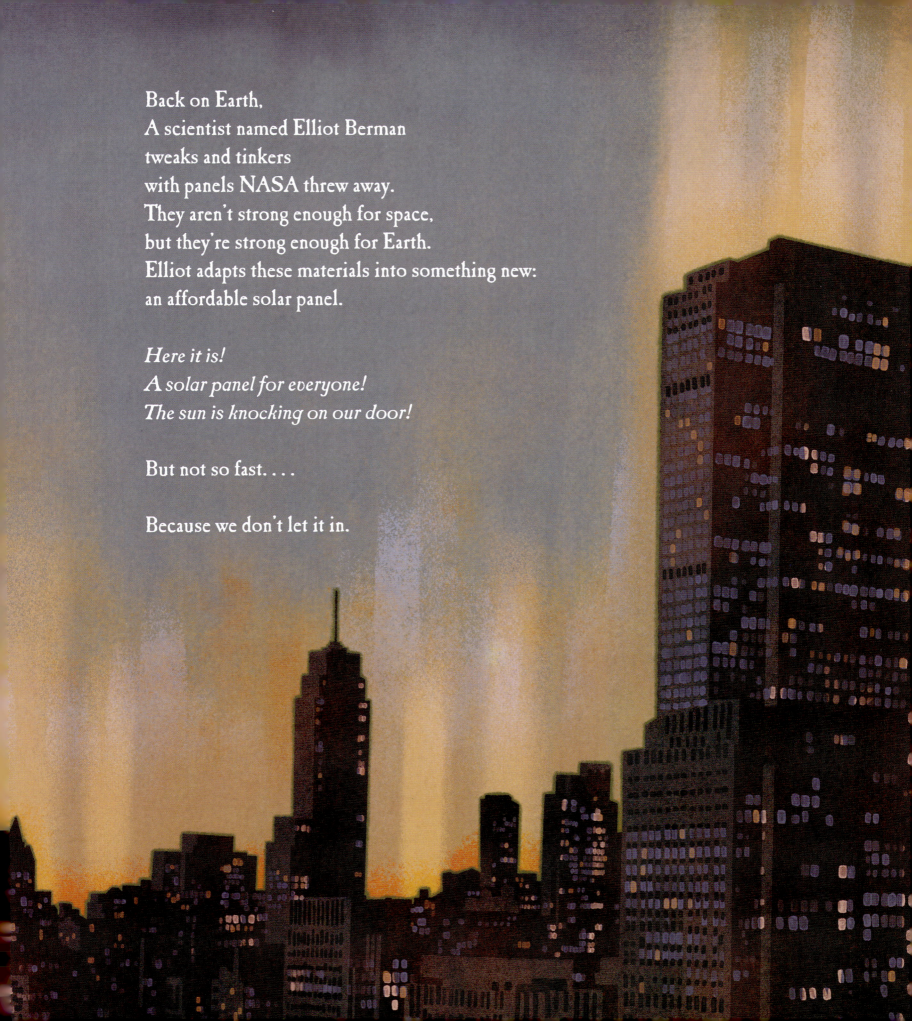

Back on Earth,
A scientist named Elliot Berman
tweaks and tinkers
with panels NASA threw away.
They aren't strong enough for space,
but they're strong enough for Earth.
Elliot adapts these materials into something new:
an affordable solar panel.

Here it is!
A solar panel for everyone!
The sun is knocking on our door!

But not so fast. . . .

Because we don't let it in.

We have turned instead
to gas for heat
and oil for electricity.
We have built our houses,
suburbs,
skyscrapers,
cities
around fossil fuels.
We no longer face the sun.

Our star feels distant,
so far away from home.

Instead of looking up,
we look down.
We unbury oil from the land.
We spill it across the sea.
We bulldoze forests
to harvest the fuel beneath.
We start wars to get more.
We hurt the Earth.
We hurt each other.

Scientists warn:
One day, we will run out of oil.
One day, we will damage the Earth beyond repair.

But not enough of us hear.

Not enough of us care.

But not for long.

During these decades,
leaders across the globe,
in Cyprus,
Greece,
Barbados,
Germany,
Denmark,
Japan,
Austria,
and Australia,
are working hard to build
and research solar energy.

Engineers in Japan
put tiny solar panels in watches,
calculators, toys,
so anyone
can hold the sun.

As global excitement grows,
A Chinese man named Shi Zhengrong
flies to an Australian university,
where he analyzes solar designs from
 around the world.
After years of study,
Zhengrong carries his knowledge home
to start the first solar company in China.

From then on,
engineers across China
tweak and tinker,
wondering,

How can we make solar power even more affordable?

Following suit,
innovators in Korea, Germany, India,
Morocco, the US, and more
experiment with new building techniques,
new materials,
new designs, until—

all these years later,
solar energy
costs less than coal.

Where does an idea start?
With wondering,
thinking,
building,
and tinkering,
until inspiration and knowledge
spread over the world
like sunlight over the horizon.

Today we are building on ideas
to make solar energy even better.
And we are asking more questions, too.

In Sweden, Greta Thunberg wonders,
How do we make our politicians listen?
She starts a climate protest and sparks a movement,
inspiring others to change the world.

In Ghana, Salma Okonkwo wonders,
How can I bring affordable power to my father's village?
She starts to build a solar farm to provide her community with both jobs and energy.

How does an idea grow?
With people bouncing off one another
like photons,
teaching and inspiring,
listening and learning.
Across the world,
we turn to one another and say,

We are incredible.

Look at all we can do.

*We reached into the sky
and carried the sun home—*

AUTHOR'S NOTE

When I started this book, I began with this question: *Who invented solar panels?* I thought there would be a simple answer, that this book would be a singular biography of one incredible person.

But as I researched, what I found instead were *many* incredible people, across the globe, across decades, all coming together.

And I learned two important lessons from this.

The first was that each individual person is important. Each person in this story—along with the many, *many* more who did not fit in these pages—was essential in developing and sharing this technology. And you are essential, too. There are many ways you can help the planet, right now, all by yourself:

Turn off the lights when you leave a room.

Don't buy things you don't need.

Write to your local politicians to remind them how important clean energy is.

All of these things will help.

But the second and even more important lesson I learned was that our true power comes when we work together, when we build off each other's ideas and knowledge and passion to make the world we want to live in.

So if you're really looking for more you can do, start conversations. Brainstorm with your parents about how you can help. Ask your teachers if you can start an environmental club at school. Talk to your friends, family, teachers, and classmates.

Because on our own, we can make the world better. But together, we can make a better world.

With care,
Tae

SOLAR ENERGY TIMELINE

c.700 BCE — Ancient Greeks build passive solar homes and bath houses with south-facing windows.

c.600 BCE — In China, people use *yangsui*, burning- or sun-mirrors, to harness solar energy. This is one of the first known tools made to use the sun's power.

c.1200 — To heat their homes with the sun, the Ancestral Pueblo people build cliff dwellings in what is now the Four Corners region of Utah, Colorado, Arizona, and New Mexico. In summer months, the cliff's overhang protects them from direct sunlight. In winter months, when the sun is lower, it shines directly into their homes.

1760–1840 — The Industrial Revolution starts in Britain and spreads across the globe, introducing steam engines and other industrial machinery in factories, which need a great deal of fossil fuels to power them.

1860 — In France, Augustin Mouchot proposes a solar steam engine.

1860–1900 — The first internal combustion engines are introduced, leading to the development of automobiles and airplanes, and expanding the use of fossil fuels.

1883 — In New York, Charles Fritts makes the first solar cells from selenium.

1891 — Clarence Kemp, in Baltimore, patents the world's first commercial solar water heater, called the Climax.

1903 — Aubrey Eneas builds his solar motor and displays it at a California ostrich farm.

1905 — Albert Einstein describes photons for the first time, which will later earn him the Nobel Prize.

1948 — Maria Telkes and Eleanor Raymond use a compound called Glauber's salt to build the first exclusively solar-heated house in Massachusetts.

1948 — In Arizona, Arthur Brown builds Rose Elementary School, the first solar-heated school.

1955 — In the United States, Bell Laboratories introduces solar panels made from silicon.

1958 — Space satellites Vanguard 1, Explorer III, Vanguard II, and Sputnik 3 launch with solar-powered systems.

1962 — Author Rachel Carson writes a book called *Silent Spring*, which raises awareness about human impact on the environment.

1960–1980 — Students, activists, and architects in California create Village Homes, a sustainable neighborhood partially inspired by the way Indigenous communities built their homes.

1967 ✺ Twenty years after his wife, Rina, first experimented with a solar-heated bathtub, Levi Yissar manufactures solar water heaters in Israel. Eventually, one in twenty homes in that country heats their water with the sun.

1968 ✺ Chemist Elliot Berman develops a cheaper silicon-based solar panel.

1971 ✺ The Soviet Union launches Salyut 1, the world's first space station, partly powered by two large solar panels.

1974 ✺ Barbados's prime minister taxes gas water heaters and encourages citizens to switch to solar heaters. About half of citizens make the switch.

1976 ✺ Greece's and Cyprus's governments invest in solar water heaters, leading to a boom in usage across the countries.

1976 ✺ A Japanese company introduces watches with rechargeable solar batteries.

1976 ✺ Denmark's government invests in a long-term renewable energy plan, which will make the country a leader in clean energy.

1977 ✺ US President Jimmy Carter puts solar panels on the White House, representing the way the US could use "the power of the sun to enrich our lives." On May 3, 1978, he declares "Sun Day," to draw attention to solar power.

1983 ✺ A group of environmentalists in Austria starts the Renewable Energy Working Group to help the public learn about, build, and use solar water heaters.

1986 ✺ US President Ronald Reagan removes the solar panels from the White House and slashes government funding for solar projects.

2000 ✺ Germany offers financial incentives to citizens who install solar panels, leading to a boom in installation across the country.

2001 ✺ Shi Zhengrong starts his solar company, Suntech, in China.

2007 ✺ Japan installs the first floating solar farm, a design that will later become popular throughout Asia.

2008 ✺ Through the National Solar Schools Program, the Australian government funds solar panel installation for thousands of schools across the country.

2009 ✺ In Japan, Tsutomu Miyasaka and his team develop the first perovskite solar panel. Perovskite is cheaper, more efficient, and can be sourced more ethically than silicon. But it's not yet stable or reliable enough for mass production.

2014 ✺ Using perovskite, researchers at Michigan State University develop the first completely transparent solar panels. They are only 1 percent as efficient as regular panels, but can be used as windows, windshields, and smartphone glass.

2016 ✸ The first solar energy plant is built in Morocco, one of the countries with the greatest potential for solar power in the world. It is the biggest solar farm yet.

2018 ✸ Greta Thunberg begins the School Strike for Climate and is joined in protest by students across the globe.

2018 ✸ Salma Okonkwo starts to build a solar park in Ghana.

2018 ✸ In Mexico, Adán Ramirez Sanchez designs a biodegradable solar panel using microalgae.

2022 ✸ In Gaza, solar panels provide Palestinians with an independent source of energy. With an estimated 12,400 rooftops, the Gaza Strip reaches the highest density of solar panels in the world.

2012–2024 ✸ Scientists in Korea, Germany, China, Saudi Arabia, Singapore, and elsewhere continue to improve perovskite solar panels, solving the previous reliability problems and creating semi-transparent panels with high efficiency.

As more and more countries across the world adopt solar and renewable energies, and as scientists continue to make breakthroughs, the future of solar is changing and developing rapidly. The sky is the limit.

FURTHER READING

Drummond, Allan. *Solar Story*. Farrar, Straus, and Giroux, 2020.

"The History of Solar." *U.S. Department of Energy: Energy Efficiency and Renewable Energy*. https://www1.eere.energy.gov/solar/pdfs/solar_timeline.pdf.

Perlin, John. *Let it Shine: The 6,000-Year Story of Solar Energy*. New World Library, 2013.

To Peter Grange,
who looked up and wondered
—T. K.

For the Sun, whose light has always guided us,
and for the children, who will illuminate the path ahead.
—R. W.

Text copyright © 2025 by Tae Keller
Illustrations © 2025 by Rachel Wada

All rights reserved
Printed in China
First Edition

For information about permission to reproduce selections from this book, write to
Permissions, W. W. Norton & Company, Inc., 500 Fifth Avenue, New York, NY 10110

For information about special discounts for bulk purchases, please contact
W. W. Norton Special Sales at specialsales@wwnorton.com or 800-233-4830

Manufacturing by Toppan Leefung
Book design by Hana Anouk Nakamura
Production manager: Delaney Adams

ISBN 978-1-324-03112-3

W. W. Norton & Company, Inc., 500 Fifth Avenue, New York, NY 10110
www.wwnorton.com

W. W. Norton & Company Ltd., 15 Carlisle Street, London W1D 3BS

1 2 3 4 5 6 7 8 9 0